# True Story

WRITTEN BY
MELISSA MONROE

ILLUSTRATED BY
MARCIN PIWOWARSKI

To My
Loves
♥

GOD'S HOLY WORD SAYS...

AND THERE WERE SHEPHERDS LIVING OUT IN THE FIELDS NEARBY, KEEPING WATCH OVER THEIR FLOCKS AT NIGHT. AN ANGEL OF THE LORD APPEARED TO THEM, AND THE GLORY OF THE LORD SHONE ALL AROUND THEM, AND THEY WERE TERRIFIED. BUT THE ANGEL SAID TO THEM,
"DO NOT BE AFRAID. I BRING YOU GOOD NEWS THAT WILL CAUSE GREAT JOY FOR ALL THE PEOPLE. TODAY IN THE TOWN OF DAVID A SAVIOR HAS BEEN BORN TO YOU; HE IS THE MESSIAH, THE LORD. THIS WILL BE A SIGN TO YOU: YOU WILL FIND A BABY WRAPPED IN CLOTHS AND LYING IN A MANGER. SUDDENLY A GREAT COMPANY OF THE HEAVENLY HOST APPEARED WITH THE ANGEL, PRAISING GOD AND SAYING, "GLORY TO GOD IN THE HIGHEST HEAVEN, AND ON EARTH PEACE TO THOSE ON WHOM HIS FAVOR RESTS." LUKE 2:8-14 (NIV)

COME READ WITH ME...

'TWAS THE EVE BEFORE CHRISTMAS MORN
THE AIR WAS QUIET AND STILL
THE LAND WAS STILL SLEEPING
NO ONE KNEW HE WOULD SOON BE HERE

FAR AWAY... FAR AWAY... THE SKY FILLED
WITH WONDER AND AWE
HEAVENLY ANGELS DANCED AND SANG
AT ALL THAT THEY FORESAW

THE SHEEP AND THE SHEPHERDS SHARED JOY
THE WORLD WOULD SOON KNOW
FINALLY... THIS WAS THE LONG-AWAITED DAY
GOD DELIVERED THIS GLOW
FINALLY... THIS WAS THE DAY GOD PROMISED LONG AGO

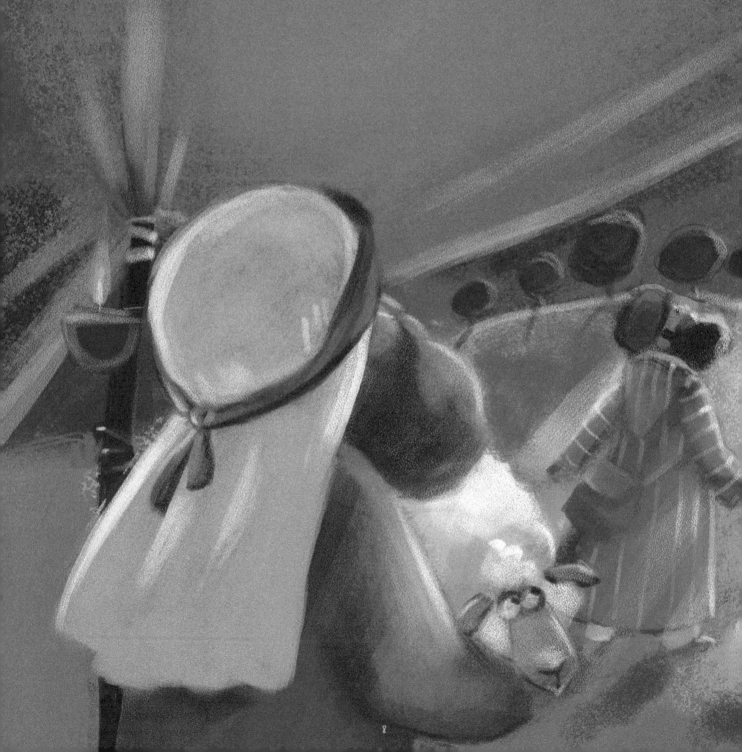

FAR AWAY... FAR AWAY...
IN THE MIDDLE OF THE NIGHT
THE MIRACLE OF ALL MIRACLES WAS BORN IN PLAIN SIGHT

THE GIFT IS A BABY
HERE TO SHOW US TRUE LOVE
HE BRINGS PEACE AND REST AND JOY
FROM HIS HEAVENLY HOME ABOVE
IF ONLY YOU COULD SEE ALL THAT HE HAS WRITTEN OF

THINK ABOUT IT... PONDER IT...
AND OPEN YOUR HEART THIS CHRISTMAS EVE
THIS IS A TRUE STORY... IT IS NOT MAKE-BELIEVE

SO... WHEN YOU LOOK IN THE SKY
AND WONDER WHAT IS TRUE
COME TO THE BABY WHO BRINGS GREAT GIFTS TO YOU

GOD'S HOLY WORD SAYS...

THE WORD BECAME FLESH AND MADE HIS DWELLING AMONG US.
WE HAVE SEEN HIS GLORY, THE GLORY OF THE ONE AND ONLY SON,
WHO CAME FROM THE FATHER, FULL OF GRACE AND TRUTH.   JOHN 1:14 (NIV)

THE SON IS THE IMAGE OF THE INVISIBLE GOD,
THE FIRSTBORN OVER ALL CREATION   COLOSSIANS 1:15 (NIV)

HE CAME AS A BABY WHO GREW AS A BOY
AND BECAME A MAN THAT SHOWED US LOVE'S EVERLASTING JOY

ABOUT THE ONE WHO SHARED THIS STORY...

MELISSA HAS SPENT HER CAREER AS A DESIGNER FOR PRIVATE AIRCRAFT, FORMERLY THE DIRECTOR OF
DESIGN FOR GULFSTREAM AEROSPACE AND NOW THE PRINCIPAL OF HER OWN DESIGN CONSULTING
PRACTICE, SHE HAS TRAVELED THE WORLD WORKING WITH FUN AND FASCINATING CLIENTS. WHILE SHE
LOVES DESIGNING AIRCRAFT FOR HER JET SETTERS, SHE FELT THE CALL TO WRITE. THIS IS ANOTHER
FULFILLING WAY TO EXPRESS HER CREATIVITY AND SHARE WITH OTHERS.
HER FAITH-FILLED LIFE IS MADE FULL BY SPENDING TIME WITH THOSE SHE LOVES AND CREATING AND
DESIGNING TO HELP OTHERS.

WESTBOW PRESS BOOKS MAY BE ORDERED THROUGH BOOKSELLERS OR BY CONTACTING:

WESTBOW PRESS
A DIVISION OF THOMAS NELSON & ZONDERVAN
1663 LIBERTY DRIVE
BLOOMINGTON, IN 47403
WWW.WESTBOWPRESS.COM
844-714-3454

COVER & INTERIOR ILLUSTRATION CREDIT:
MARCIN PIWOWARSKI

ISBN: 978-1-6642-6976-7 (SC)
ISBN: 978-1-6642-6978-1 (HC)
ISBN: 978-1-6642-6977-4 (E)

LIBRARY OF CONGRESS CONTROL NUMBER: 2022911446

PRINT INFORMATION AVAILABLE ON THE LAST PAGE.

WESTBOW PRESS REV. DATE 07/26/2022

WESTBOW
PRESS®
A DIVISION OF THOMAS NELSON
& ZONDERVAN

Printed in the USA
CPSIA information can be obtained
at www.ICGtesting.com
LVHW061944260923
759380LV00003B/56